From the BEGINNING

BURDON-CAMPBELL

From the Beginning

PROMINENT
BOOKS
EDGE

5830 E 2nd St, Ste 7000 #9983
Casper, WY 82609
USA

This book is dedicated to my mother Ella Campbell,
And in memory of my father Isaac Campbell.
"Good Samaritans"

FOREWORD

I volunteered to conduct an orientation class for youth and young adult members of my church. When I began the class, I realized the need for a book that would guide them to answers they needed.

Even youth who were raised in the church Sunday schools, and knew all the stories of Noah's Ark, the Three Wise Men, and Jesus on the cross, began to question at age thirteen to fifteen: (A.) "Why didn't God write The Bible Himself?" (B.) Does God really talk to you? (C.) "Why can't we have fun in here?" At this age, the youth are too old for children's church and not equipped to understand the sermons, so they write notes and play tic tack toe.

At ages sixteen to seventeen, they come to church only because it is a family thing. At age eighteen to twenty, they are moving away from home, and hopefully taking with them the values learned in youth Sunday school.

At age twenty-four and up, the hard knocks of life will bring them back to church searching for guidance. Surely not all youth and young adults will follow this path.

This book is designed to assist new members in finding answers to their questions, to introduce Bible history, and to offer awareness of how God organized the church.

I would like to encourage you to grow as a true Christian, and I pray that this book provides a blessing to all who read it.

October, 2002 Burdon Campbell

LINK TO THE ANCIENT WORLD

In 1947, near the Dead Sea, fifteen miles east of Jerusalem, two Bedouin shepherd boys happened upon a hillside cave, while searching for a lost goat. The shepherd boys entered the cave and found pottery jars twenty to twenty-five inches high and ten inches wide.

Inside the jars were leather scrolls wrapped in squares of cloth and covered with a black sticky substance.Because of a war between the Arabs and the Jews, the scientific investigation of the cave did not begin until February 1949.

The name "Dead Sea Scrolls" was given to the ancient manuscripts found in a number of caves west of the Dead Sea. The Dead Sea Scrolls include two scrolls of Isaiah-one was complete-and most of the first two books of Habakkuk, and many fragments of manuscripts of the books of Psalms, Jeremiah, and Daniel.

The scrolls were deposited in the caves 2,000 years before their discovery in 1947. The discovery of the Dead Sea Scrolls is the link to the original Bible.

ACKNOWLEDGMENTS

Thank you, God, for your inspiration and for providing a lamp to my feet and a light for my path. I must collectively say **Thank You** to **Reuben Pringle** and myother family members, and brothers and sisters in Christ, for their encouragement, support, and love. You gave me words of assurance that kept me going when I thought of stopping.

To my best friend, **Israel "Juan" Gaines** who spent countless hours helping me to make this dream a reality. **Thank you!**

A very special **Thank You to Carl D. Smith,** who replanted an old seed; to my wife **Mary L .,** who turned the soil and added water; to Pastor Donnie Bryant, who said, "Come grow in the light of Jesus Christ!"; to **Pastor Roselee Charley**, who trimmed the branches and encouraged strong growth.

"The fruit of this vine is God's Gift."

> *When I was a child, I spoke as a child, I understood as a child, I thought as a child; but when I became a man, I put away childish things.*
> *1 Corinthians 13:11*

THE BIBLE TAKES SHAPE

One Sunday while driving home after church, it was raining very hard; the sky was almost black, my five-year-old son pressed his face against the window, trying to look straight up, then said, "Dad, if God lives in heaven, how can he watch over us today?" my wife and I laughed and gave him an answer that satisfied his curiosity.

"God can see through clouds son."

Now I have a nine-year-old granddaughter, who came to me with a question that took her fifteen minutes to pose. Finally, after assuring me that she truly loved God and his son Jesus, she said "Grandpa, how did The Bible get started? When God created us, who wrote what happened? Could the slaves read or write? Does God talk to people today?"

As a teenager, I had similar questions cross my mind also; to some I got the standard "Have faith" answer, and the others I dared not to ask. Over the years, I have talked to many Sunday school teachers from various classes (ages eleven to sixteen). Most of their students had attended Sunday school all their life, some were attending Christian schools, and a few were new believers. The teachers all heard the same question at one time or another: Where did The Bible come from?

To better understand how stories and concepts were passed down from ancient history without a loss in content or purpose due to translation, we must compare our history to our present time.

In 1000 BC, the purpose of The Bible was to spread The Word of God, teaching people how to love God and one another. Through all the translations, improvements, and versions, the purpose of The Bible today is still to spread The Word of God, teaching man how to love God and one another.

In 1885, Karl Benz designed and built the world's first automobile powered by a gas engine. The purpose of the automobile was to provide transportation. In spite of all the improvements that have occurred, the purpose of the automobile today is still to provide transportation.

Although The Bible originated in the Middle East, it has been translated into more than 290 languages and dialects. More than 30 million copies of The Bible are sold each year. Hotels and motels in the United States provide Bibles in each room at no cost.

The Bible is a collection of sixty-six books, written over a 1,500-year period by various authors from all walks of life, from shepherds to kings. The authors were all guided in their thinking and writing by The Holy Spirit. The sixty-six works are fundamentally unified in theme and contents.

> "For prophecy never came by the will of man, but holy men of God spoke as they were moved by The Holy Spirit."
> (2Peter 1:21 NKJV)

The Bible is divided into two main sections: The Old Testament and The New Testament. The people of The Old Testament told and retold the stories of God's interaction with the Israelites.

Around 100 BC, The Old Testament was written, first in the Hebrew language on animal skins (called vellum) or on papyrus (a paper made from the papyrus plant).

Because The Testament is the sacred The Word of God, the scribes carefully preserved every letter and word of the original text when making copies. In the sixth century AD, Jewish scholars called masoretes added a system of vowels to the consonants of the Hebrew text to preserve the pronunciation and meaning of the text.

The New Testament was first written in the Greek language. The first four books recount the life of Jesus Christ and His ministry, His death, and His resurrection.

Because many of the same events and teachings appear in the books of Matthew, Mark, and Luke, those books are called the Synoptic Gospels. The term "synoptic gospel" indicates that all three disciples viewed the same event with the same point of view.

The book of John often relates events and sayings of Jesus which are not found in the other three books, which indicates that the other three disciples were not present.

THE CANON

The word canon is a translation of the Greek word kanon, which comes from the Hebrew word keneh, meaning "straight rod" or "ruler" or "measuring stick," the standard by which something could be measured. The presence of false books and writings made it necessary to carefully review each book.

The Canon determined which books were accepted as being the inspired Word of God. This decision was not made by one person, or one single group of people at any one point in history. This process took many centuries. The New Testament reached its final form in AD 397.

The test for canonization asks five questions:

1. Authorship - Does it come from God?
2. Prophetic - Was it written by a man of God?
3. Authentic - Does it tell the truth about God and man?
4. Dynamic - Does it convey the life of God?
5. Was it received, used, and accepted by the people of God?

OVERVIEW

The Old Testament is divided into five groups: The Law, History, Poetic Books, Major Prophets and Minor Prophets. The period covers from creation to about 400 BC.

The period between The Old Testament and The New Testament is commonly known as the "400 silent years."

The New Testament is also divided into five groups: The Gospels, History, Pauline Epistle, General Epistle, and Prophecy.

The Old Testament

The first five books of The Old Testament are a distinct unit called The Law.

The Law defines: (1.) Israel's relationship with God, (2.) the Israelites' relationship with one another, (3.) and their relationship with outsiders.

Genesis, chapters 1 to 11 covers Creation, the fall of man, and the growth of the nation. In Genesis chapter 12, God chose Abraham to be father of the great nation.

The rest of Genesis is the story of Abraham and his descendants, Isaac, Jacob, and Joseph, and the birth of the Jews.

Genesis	**Leviticus**
Exodus	**Numbers**
Deuteronomy	

Exodus chapter 20:2-7 summarizes God's laws that teach us how to love God and one another (The Ten Commandments).

Exodus, Leviticus, Numbers, and **Deuteronomy** contain laws that explain how the principles of The Ten Commandments were to be applied in Israel:

1. For the worshiping of God,
2. For governing the nation,
3. For individual behavior,
4. For social interaction,

The next twelve books of The Old Testament are a distinct unit, called **History**.

These books tell the history of Israel from the time the nation entered The Promised Land until about 400 BC.

These books show us how The Lord brought thechosen people into the Promised Land, and tells the stories of the leaders and kings of Israel.

The next five books of The Old Testament are called the **Poetic Books.**

Joshua	1 Samuel	1 Chronicles
Judges	2 Samuel	2 Chronicles
Ruth	1 Kings	Ezra
2 Kings	Nehemiah	
Esther		

Job	Proverbs
Psalms	Ecclesiastes
Song of Songs	

These are books of encouragement, comfort, wisdom, and songs. They have much to say about the problem of suffering, the need for praise, and how to live daily in relation with **God**.

The next seventeen books of The Old Testament are books of **Prophets,** which are divided into two sections, the "**major**" and the "**minor**" prophets.

They are called"major" and "minor" because of the amount of material contained in each book. The major prophets had more to say than the minor prophets.

Through the prophets, God warned Israel that if they did not turn away from sin, and worship and obey him, then He would judge them harshly. These prophets lived from about 749 to 540 BC.

Fourteen letters are called **Pauline epistles,** because Paul was the author. Seven of the letters are called General epistles, because they were written to the church at large.

The last book of The New Testament is called the **Prophecy.**

Revelation means an unveiling or disclosure. Revelation is the only New Testament book t**hat focuses primarily on prophetic events, and refers to itself as a prophetic book**.

It is the only book that specifically promises a blessing to those **who read it.**

Minor Prophets			
Hosea	Joel	Amos	Obadiah
Jonah	Micah	Nahum	Habakkuk
Zephaniah		Haggai	Zechariah
Malachi			

Major Prophets	
Isaiah	Lamentations
Jeremiah	Ezekiel
	Daniel

The New Testament

The first four books of The New Testament are called **The Gospels.**

These gospels recount the life of Jesus Christ, showing how Jesus fulfilled the prophecies of The Old Testament.

They trace His genealogy, baptism, message,miracles, death, resurrection, and His great commission to all of His disciples.

The next book of The New Testament is called History.

The *book of Acts,* written by Luke, is an account of the early church as it grew from a small band of disciples into a group of believers spreading throughout the Roman Empire. Acts focuses on Peter's work with the Jews, and Paul's work with the Gentiles.

The next twenty-one books of The New Testament are called **Epistles, or (letters).**

Epistles refers to the twenty-one (letters) of The New Testament, written by five authors. Paul wrote fourteen, John wrote three, Peter wrote two, James, and Jude each wrote one.

The letters began with the name of the author, the addressee, words of greeting, and then the message of the letter. At the end, the author usually gave his name.

Matthew	Mark	Luke
	John	

ACTS

Pauline Epistle

Roman	Philippians	2 Timothy
1 Corinthians	Colossians	Titus
2 Corinthians	1 Thessalonians	Philemon
Galatians	2 Thessalonians	Hebrews
Ephesians	1 Timothy	

General Epistle

James	1 John	Jude
1 Peter	2 John	
2 Corinthians	3 John	

Revelation

"Blessed is he who reads and those who hear the words of this prophecy, and keep those things which are written in it, for the time is near."

(Revelation 1:3 NKJV)

And curse to those who add or detract from it:

"For I testify to everyone who hears the words of the prophecy of this book: If anyone adds to these things, God will add to him the plagues that are written in this book, and if anyone takes away from the words of the book of this prophecy, God shall take away his part from The Book of Life, from the holy city, and from the things which are written in this book"

(Revelation 22:18-19 NKJV)

Revelation addresses three major unveilings:

"Things you have seen" - Chapter 1
"Things that are now happening" - Chapters 2-3
"Things that will happen later" - Chapters 4-22.

REVIEW

1. What three major unveiling does the book of Revelation address?

2. What book of The Bible makes a specific promise? What is that promise?
3. *Twenty-one* books of The Bible are called Epistles. What is an epistle?
4. Name three General Epistles.
5. The test for canonization asks five questions. What are the first three questions?
6. The Bible is a collection of sixty-six books. How many books are in The Old Testament?
7. Name the five books of The Bible called The Law.
8. Name the books that are called The Gospels.
9. In what language was The New Testament first written?
10. 10. In what language was The Old Testament first written?

CHOOSING YOUR BIBLE

We live in the age of printing machines, copy machines, and computers, and it can be hard to imagine that each book of The Bible was written by hand.

Without an easy or an efficient way to make copies of The Bible, the written Word of God was practically unknown to the common people during the early growth of the English Bible.

In 1382, John Wyclif, an English scholar and Bible student, gave the English their first complete Bible in their language. He translated The New Testament into common English. After his death in 1384, his friends completed his work

William Tyndale, an English translator, was determined that the English common people should have The Bible in their own language. He translated The New Testament in 1525 and the first five books of The Old Testament in 1530.

In 1604, King James I of England decided there needed to be a version of The Bible written in the language of his time. He ordered a new translation to be made, based on the Greek and Hebrew manuscripts.

The outcome was known as the King James Version of 1611. Between 1604 and today, the English language has grown, and our life and lifestyles have grown and changed. Even the King James

Version has had many revisions while maintaining the content and unified theme of The Bible.

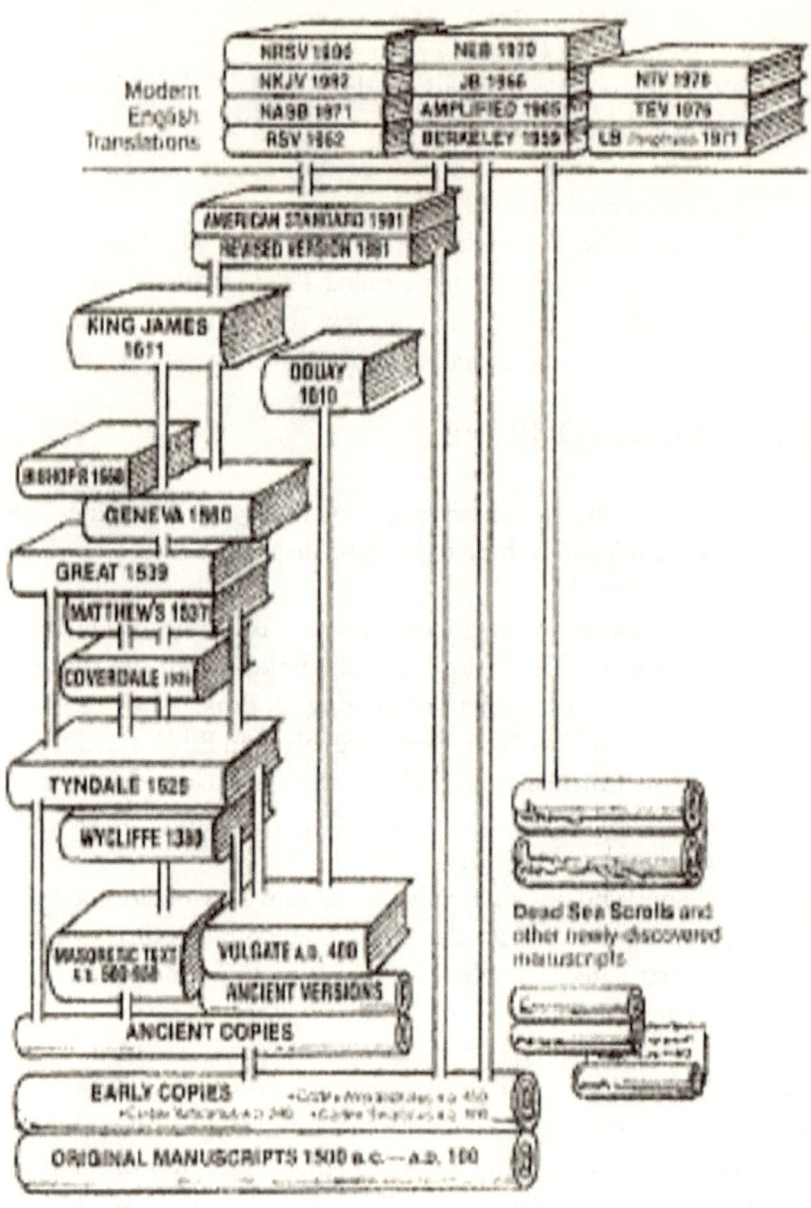

Thompson Chain - Reference Study Bible NIV October 1997
With the permission of Kirkbride Bible Company
Today there are more than fourteen English versions of The Bible, and most are held to the standards of the King James Version.

<u>Version</u>

King James Version (KJV)
New King James Version (NKJV)
New American Standard Version (NASB)
New International Version (NIV)
Revised Standard Version (RSV)
New Revised Standard (RSV)
The Living Bible (LB)
New Living Translation (NLT)
New Century Version (NCV)
The Message (TM)
Amplified Bible (AB)
Revised English Bible (REB)
Good News Bible: Today's English Version (TEV)
God's Word (GD)

Translators today, normally use one of three techniques when translating:

The **Word-for-Word technique**
The **Thought-for-Thought concept technique**
The **Paraphrase technique**

The word-for-word technique changes yesterday's language to today's language (Example: changing thee and thine to you and your).

The thought concept technique translates the concept of the text from yesterday to today, **thought for thought.**

The paraphrase technique is to say in other words without changing the meaning.

Using the King James Version of Ephesians 2:8-9, compare the version:

King James Version (KJV)

"For by grace you have been saved through faith, and that not of yourselves: it is the gift of God: Not of works, lest anyone should boast."

New King James (NKJV)

"For by grace you have been saved through faith, and that not of yourselves: it is the gift of God: not of works, lest anyone should boast."

(Word-for-Word)

New International Version (NIV)

"For it is by grace you have been saved, through faith and this not from yourselves it is the gift of God-not by works so no one can boast."

(Thought-for-Thought)

New Living Translation (NIV)

"God saved you by his special favor when you believed. And you cannot take credit for this: it is a gift from God. Salvation is not a reward for the good things we have done, so none of us con boast about it."

(Paraphrase)

In addition to the personal devotional Bibles, there are study Bibles, reference Bibles, Bible dictionaries, and children's Bibles. There are also surveys of the authors, study guides, maps, archaeological discoveries, chronology timelines, and charts. Most Bibles (depending on the version) will contain a combination of all those features.

The Bible is now found on audiotapes, on computer programs, and on the Internet. Your choice of Bible depends mainly on a translation with which you are comfortable. Discuss your choices with other believers to get a feel for what you need. Whatever translation you choose, continue to read and study your Bible.

Thank God for today's technology. It took a lifetime for our ancestors to gain the knowledge that we have at our fingertips.

USING YOUR BIBLE

At some point in time, you have heard or you will hear someone quote a Bible verse that does not sound right or it sounds too good. Many times, if one word is omitted or added to a verse, it will change its meaning.

During a sermon, most pastors or ministers will say, "Turn to book *** chapter ** verse"" and read," because all Christians must read The Bible so that they know the truth of God's Word.

Most of the time, when The Bible is misquoted, it is not done purposely to mislead us; however, The Bible does warn us;

> *"But there were also false prophets among the people, even as there will be false teachers among you, who will secretly bring in destructive heresies, even denying The Lord who bought them, and bring on themselves swift destruction."*
> *(2Peter 2:1 NKJV)*

The Bibles of today feature the words of Christ in red ink, concordance references, cross-references, index to subject, index to topics, index to the miracles of Jesus, index to the parables of Jesus, out-

13

line of Bible history, and outline of each book of The Bible. The most important feature of any Bible is its concordance and cross-references.

The concordance allows you to find a verse in The Bible by using a key word from that verse. It will also reference every verse in The Bible that contains that keyword.

Example A: A popular and often misquoted Bible verse:

"Money is the root of all evil."

Using the concordance, look under the key word money, we find the verse is 1 Timothy 6:10 (NIV), which actually reads:

> *"For the love of money is a root of all kinds of evil. Some people eager for money have wandered from the faith and pierced themselves with many grief,"*

Other key words that could be used to find that verse are <u>love</u> or <u>root</u>.

Example B: Another popular Bible quote:

> *"So in everything, do to others what you would have them do to you, for this sums up the law and the prophets."*

If misquoted, it could be difficult to find, due to the lack of key words in the verse. However, using the key word **law** and **prophets**, we find the verse in *Matthew 7:12 and Luke 6:31.*

The concordance references every verse that contains that key word.

<u>EXAMPLE: KEY WORD BRIDE</u>

<u>Concordance</u>

BRIBE
Exodus 23:8 **do not accept a b.**

Deuteronomy 16:19 **for a b blinds the eyes of the wise**
Deuteronomy 27:25 **Cursed is the man who accepts a b**
Proverb 6:35 will refuse the b, **however great it BRIDE**
Isaiah 62:5 as a bridegroom rejoices over his b, Revelation 19:7
and his b has made herself ready Revelation 21:2 *as a b beautifully dressed.*

Revelation 21:9 I **will show you the b, the wife Revelation 22:17 The Sprit and the b say, Co**
BRIDEGROOM

Psalm 19:5 which is like a B coming forth
Matthew 25:1 I and went out to meet the b
Matthew 25:5 the b was a long time in coming
EXAMPLE: KEY WORD TAX.

Concordance

TAX (TAXES)

Matthew 11:19 **a friend of t collectors and sinners**
Matthew 17:34 **of the two drachma t came to Peter**
TAXES (TAX)

Matthew 22:17 is it right to pay t to Caesar or not
Romans 13:7 If you owe T, pay t, if revenue,
The Cross-reference, sometimes referred to as the Cyclopedia, normally appears in the center column. It will also allow us to reference a verse to other verses by Subject concept.

Example: John 2:22

<u>The verse The Reference</u>

21 But the temple He had spoken of was His body

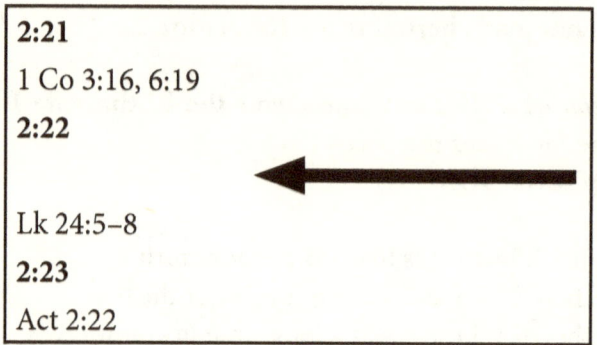

2:21
1 Co 3:16, 6:19
2:22

Lk 24:5–8
2:23
Act 2:22

22 After He was raised from the dead, his disciples recalled What He had said. Then they believed The Scriptures and The Words that Jesus had spoken. 23 Now while He was in Jerusalem at the Passover Feast, many people saw the Miraculous signs He was doing and believed in His name when they saw the signs which He did.

Luke 24:5 8 is the reference by subject of John 2:22.

The above is a very brief outline of Bible history. You are encouraged to research more into Bible history or perhaps trace the life of one of its authors, or use a systematic outline to read your Bible through in one year.

Now that we have covered a very brief outline of a document (Bible) that begins with:

"In the beginning God created the heavens and the earth"

Take some quiet time and think about what it must have been like to live in the year 1000 BC. Just think about how The Bible was passed from generation to generation by word of mouth. It has been translated into most of the major languages without a change in theme or content.

Every society has adopted a portion of The Ten Commandments. The biblical concept that applied in 1000 BC continues to apply today. The Bible is man's guide to life, the relationship between God and man, and between man and man. Truly, this is The Word of God.

STUDYING THE WORD

The foundation of a Christian's life is Bible study. God speaks to us through His Word, ('The Bible). If we have not read or studied The Bible, then we cannot know what God is saying to us. Bible study guides our spiritual life as well as our day-to-day life.

Five important principles of Bible study are:

- A. Be consistent: (As we feed our bodies daily, we must also feed our minds spiritually daily.)
- B. Study The Bible in context: (To study one verse
- C. at a time is like reading only the newspaper headlines)
- D. Know who is speaking.
- E. Know who is being spoken to.
- F. Know the subject of the speaker. [Study the entire chapter in order to understand the whole story in context.)

There are three methods of Bible study;

Passive Bible study
Active Bible study
Self Bible study

Passive Bible study: The traditional Wednesday night Bible study is aclass of ten to forty-plusmembers. The deacons lead the devotion and the opening and closing prayer. The teacher selects the subject, and the classes are normally taught in a lecture format.

Active Bible study is a class of not more than eight to ten members. The students, on a rotational basis, will conduct the devotion, and the opening and closing prayer. The subject is predetermined, using a study guide or The Bible as a textbook. Prior to class, the teacher assigns a reading assignment for each student, and the student presents the assignment to the class and conducts an open discussion with the class.

Example: The subject of study is the book of Job, Student A is assigned *chapter 1*, Student B is assigned *chapter 2*, and so on. Student A presents *chapter 1* to the class and then conducts the open discussion. *Students A* and *B* must also be prepared to take part in the discussion of the remaining *chapters*. The teacher acts as advisor and guides the open discussion.

Self Bible study:

Use a systematic Bible study guide, or choose the subject from an event that has or is occurring in your life.

Use the concordance to find a verse that reflects on the subject you want to study.

Establishing a quiet time is a <u>must</u>. Finding an hour of quiet time in today's life can be difficult. If you cannot manage to find sixty minutes a day, then try thirty or fifteen minutes twice a day.

Begin this quiet time with a prayer for guidance. Relax, open your heart and mind, and let God nourish you while meditating on the verse you are studying. Read the verse carefully.

Write the verse in your own words, then read the complete chapter. To gain a better understanding may require the reading of the *chapter* before and after the *verse*.

Many times, you may not clearly understand the verses, however, continue to concentrate on what God has already revealed to you, and then trust God to make all that which is vague clear.

As you read, listen with your heart and mind as God speaks through The Bible in one of four tones.

Training tone - training in right living.
Teaching tone - teaching the faith.
Rebuking tone - correcting errors.
Correcting tone - resetting the direction of a life.

Question yourself about what you have read. Is there a command to obey? Is there a promise to claim? Is there a change to be made in your life? And is there a parable providing a vision of life?

Answering these questions may be difficult at first, but it will become easier as God's Word comes into your life.

The advantage of passive Bible study

The lecture format can be highly motivating and provide guidance. The students have an opportunity to listen to others, to ask questions, to get a clearer understanding of the subject, to give a testimony, and fellowship with other Christians.

The advantage of active Bible study

Studying in a small group provides closeness and intimate sharing of God's Word, and share experiences about the relationship with God and each other. Under the guidance of the teacher, the students are conducting the class and improving public speaking, public prayer, and teaching skills.

The advantage of self Bible study

This is an option for students whose life schedule will not allow time for the traditional Wednesday night study classes. At some point, all members must self-study and pray in order to establish a personal relationship with God.

There is no disadvantage in Bible study.

Bible study is not limited in structure or night of the week. Those of you who have odd life schedules need to talk to others and share your need for a Bible study class. Your deacons will be happy to help organize and provide guidance for any type of study group needed.

"For where two or three are gathered together
in My name, I am there in their midst."
(Matthew 18:20 NKJV)

EXERCISE

1. Using the concordance and your Bible, find this verse:

"Be diligent to present yourself approved to God, a worker who does not need to be ashamed,

The *verse* is found in
The_Testament
Book of
Chapter Verse
The key word is

2. The correct reading of this *verse* is?

From the above *verse*:

1. Who is speaking?
2. Who is he speaking to ?
3. What is the subject?
4. Using the concordance and your Bible, find this verse; "When He had been baptized, Jesus came up *immediately from the water; and behold the heavens were opened to Him, and He saw The Spirit of God descending like a dove and alighting upon Him."*

Book_____Chapter_____Verse_____

5. Using the cross-reference, find two verses which reference the above verse by subject.

Book_____Chapter_____Verse_____

Book_____Chapter_____Verse_____

6. In 1611, The Bible was translated to English using Greek and Hebrew manuscripts. Today that Bible translation is known as the_____

7. The five principles of Bible study are

A.

B.

C.

D.

E.

PRAYER

Between ages nine and fourteen, I spent every summer in Houston, Texas with my grandmother. You may have heard the stories about the Southern grandmothers who put their grandchildren on drugs. They DRUG them to Sunday school and DRUG them to church.

My grandmother also DRUG my sister and me to usher board meetings, choir practice, and Bible study. I remember at the end of one of those Bible studies, everyone was standing, hand-in-hand, and heads bowed,

The Bible study leader asked, "Sister Walton, (my grandmother) would you close us out with a prayer?"Grandmother turned to her best friend and asked, "Sister Dillenham, would you pick up the cross?" Sister Dillenham began to pray.

I now understand that this was grandmother's polite way of saying, "I do know how to pray, but I do not like to pray in public. I am not a public speaker."

God made us all a little different from one another, some are extrovert, (outgoing) and some are introverted, (shy). Some of us are singers and others enjoy the music.

In the beginning, I was much like my grandmother. However, the more I learned about prayer made it easier to pray. There are still times that I am not comfortable with public prayer, but I carry on. **Jesus teaches us to pray in private,**

> *"But you, when you pray, go into your room, and when you have shut your door, pray to your Father who is in the secret place; and your Father who sees in secret will reward you openly."*
> **(Matthew 6:6 NKJV)**

Jesus also teaches His disciples a public prayer.

> "So He said to them, 'When you pray, say:
> Our Father in heaven,
> Hallowed be Your name.
> Your will be done
> On earth as it is in heaven
> Give us day by day our daily bread.
> And forgive us our sins,
> For we also forgive everyone who is indebted
> LO US.
> And do not lead us into temptation, but
> deliver us from the evil one"
> (Luke 11:2-4 NKJV)

A personal relationship is developed through communication. God communicates with us through His Holy Bible. We communicate with God through prayer. Through Bible study and prayer, we establish a personal relationship with God.

> *"If you abide in Me, and My words abide in you, you will ask what you desire, and it shall be done for you."*
> **(John 15:7 NKJV)**

Private prayer is between you and God in your private place.

> *"And when you pray, you shall not be like the hypocrites. For they love to pray standing in the synagogues and on the corners of the streets, that they may be seen by men. Assuredly, I say to you, they have their reward. But you, when you pray, go into your room, and when you have shut your door, pray to your Father who is in the secret place; and your Father who sees in secret will reward you openly."*
> **(Matthew 6:5- 8 NKJV)**

Your prayers:

1. do not require a proper word
2. have no rules to pray by
3. are not limited to place, posture, or time of day.

When praying, we must:

1. have Faith "Complete faith in God"
2. have Obedience "obey God fully and completely"
3. Be patient

Wait patiently on God, we are all on His time schedule. We must know that prayer is not effective if we harbor a bitter spirit.

> *"And whenever you stand praying, if you have anything against anyone, forgive him that your Father in heaven may also forgive you your trespasses."*
> **(Mark 11:25 NKJV)**

Pray in private, while walking, riding, or playing. The song in your heart may become a prayer of thanksgiving. Example:

"I just want to thank You, Forever and ever and ever, For all You have done for me, Blessing and honor and glory, They all belong to You, *Thank You, Jesus, for blessing me.*"

Basically, prayer is simply talking to God just like you would talk to your best friend. Praise God; give Him all the glory, then thank Him for what He has done for you. Tell Him what is on your heart, your problems, then ask for His help and guidance.

Prayer is also public

There are times in ministry that require public prayer, to open and close meetings, praying for guidance.

> *"When we had come to the end of those days, we departed and went on our way; and they all accompanied us, with wives and children, till we were out of the city. And we knelt down on the shore and prayed. When we had taken our leave of one another, we boarded the ship, and they returned home."*
> **(Act 21:5 6 NKJV)**

Jesus sometimes prayed aloud for the benefit of those present.

> *"Then they took away the stone from the place where the dead man was laying. And Jesus lifted up His eyes and said 'Father, I thank You that You have heard Me And I know that You always hear Me, but because of the people who are standing by I said this, that they may believe that You sent Me."*
> **(John 11:41-42 NKJV)**

Praying in public can be a little uncomfortable for the newcomer; however, the newcomer needs to know that we pray from

the heart. In Acts 21:5-6, the prayer was organized. All the disciples, their wives and children knelt down to pray. Today we are also organized by the instruction, "every head bowed" or "every eye closed" or "everyone touch one another"; now one voice prays for all.

The disciples asked Jesus: Lord, teach us to pray!

> *"Now it came to pass, as Jesus was praying in a certain place, when He ceased, that one of His disciples said to Him, 'Lord, teach us to pray, as John also tought his disciples.'"*
> **(Luke 11:1 NKJV)**

The Lord's Prayer is treasured by Christians. It appears everywhere in church life (Luke 11:2-4 NKJV).

Today we can use The Lord's Prayer as a model to organize public prayer.

Every eye closed and heads bowed is one method of organization
(Luke 11:2-4 NKJV)

Our Father in heaven,

Approach God as our Father, Keep in mind that one voice is praying for all.

Hallowed be Your name. Your kingdom come. Your will be done. On earth as it is in heaven.

Acknowledge God's powers, Ruler of heaven and earth, our creator, His will which is for our good, be done on earth.

Praise God, give Himn all the honor and glory for what He has done.

Give us day by day our daily bread,

Ask God to give us what we need, His help, His guidance, His healing, and His blessing.

And do not lead us into temptation, but deliver us from the evil one.

<u>Ask for direction</u>, guide us, keep us from failing when tested, help us to know the right things to do, protect us from evil that await us in life.
Amen.

Do not expect God to answer in some divine way or somehow speak in a loud voice from the heavens. God speaks to us through His Word. God speaks to our hearts and to our minds. God speaks to our sense of moral righteousness, fairness, and to our sense of what is right. God also speaks to us through other believers. When Jesus Christ is dwelling within, God talks constantly to our conscience, soul, and spirit.

Through the communication of Bible study and prayer, we build a personal relationship with God.

THE WORKING CHURCH TODAY

The term church is the English translation of the Greek word ECCLESIA (Eh-Klee-zhee-uh) which means "called out" or to indicate an "assembly."

Jesus Christ established the church during his ministry and under His authority, He gave His promise of perpetuity and blessing.

> "And I also say to you that you are Peter, and on this rock I will build My church, and the gates of Hades shall not prevail against it. And I will give you the keys of the kingdom of heaven, and whatever you bind on earth will be bound in heaven, and whatever you loose on earth will be loosed in heaven."
> **(Matthew 16;18 19 NKJV)**

The New Testament describes the church as a body of believers, professing trust in Jesus Christ, meeting together to worship Him, and seeking to enlist others to become His followers The church is a group of Christian people, not simply the building where Christian people meet.

In a letter to the church, Paul uses the human body to describe features of church life. He emphasizes the responsibility of Christians to share their gifts with the body of the church.

"For by one Spirit we were all baptized into one body-whether Jews or Greeks, whether slaves or free-and have all been made to drink into one Spirit."

(1Corinthians 12:13 NKJV)

"But now indeed there are many members, yet one body. And the eye cannot say to the hand, 'I have no need of you'; nor again the head to the feet, I have no need of you.' No, much rather, those members of the body which seem to be weaker are necessary. And those members of the body which we think to be less honorable, on *these we bestow greater honor; and our unpresentable parts have greater modesty, but our presentable parts have no need. But God composed the body, having given greater honor to that part which lacks it, that there should be no schism in the body, but that the members should have the same care for one another. And if one member suffers all the members suffer with it; or if one member is honored, all the members rejoice with it. Now you are the body of Christ, and members individually. And God has appointed these in the church: first apostles, second prophets, third teachers, after that miracles, then gifts of healings, helps, administrations, varieties of tongues."*

(1Corinthians 12:20-28 NKJV)

Today, the church continues to be a self governed body of individuals having equal rights, privileges, and duties. Although it is not complex in its organization, it is probably the oldest and purest form of democracy. The church constitution and bylaws are the written laws and principles that govern the church's affairs The constitution and bylaws also provide the votes that give the members a voice in the church's mission, goals, and direction.

The Church History. The Church Covenant.

The Church Mission and Purpose.

The Church Constitution and Bylaws.

Young adults and new members should become familiar with these documents.

When selecting leaders and officers of the church, the church must adhere to the guidelines in The Bible, which clearly defines the qualification, duties, and role of church leaders and officers. This shows that Jesus wanted His church to be governed on earth.

The Pastor Officers

The term pastor is a translation from the Greek term "poimen," which means shepherd. Jesus set the standards for all shepherds, and is referred to as The Great Shepherd:

> *"Now may The God of peace who brought up*
> *our Lord Jesus from the dead, that great Shepherd*
> *of the sheep."*
>
> **(Hebrews 13:20 NKJV).**

"And I will give you shepherds according to My heart, who will feed you with knowledge and understanding."

A pastor is considered a spiritual shepherd, a man or woman called by God to preach the gospel and serve as church leader and overseer.

> *"And I will give you shepherds according to My heart, who will feed you with knowledge and understanding."*
>
> **(Jeremiah 3:15 NKJV)**

The qualifications of pastor are clearly defined as a man or woman above reproach.

> *"A bishop [overseer] then must be blameless, the husband of one wife, temperate, sober- minded, of good behavior, hospitable, able to teach; not given to wine, not violent, not greedy for money, but gentle, not quarrelsome, not covetous; one who rules his own house well, having his children in submission with all reverence (for if a man does not know how to rule his own house, how will he take care of the church of God?); not a novice, lest being puffed up with pride he fall into the same condemnation as the devil. Moreover he must have a good testimony among those who are outside, lest he fall into reproach and the snare of the devil.*
>
> **(1 Timothy 3:2-7 NKJV)**

The duty of a pastor is to feed his/her sheep, strengthening the feeble, bandaging the hurt, bringing back those driven away, and seeking those who are lost.

> *"Son of man, prophesy against the shepherds of Israel, prophesy and say to them, 'Thus says The Lord God to the shepherds: Woe to the shepherds of*

Israel who feed themselves! Should not the shepherds feed the flocks?"

(Ezekiel 34:2 NKJV)

The weak you have not strengthened, nor have you healed those who were sick, nor bound up the broken, nor brought back what was driven away, nor sought what was lost, but with force and cruelty you have ruled them.

(Ezekiel 34:4 NKJV)

The Dencon and Deaconess

The term "deacon" is a translation of the Greek word DIAKONOS, which translates to servant or minister.

The term deaconess is not the deacon's wife; the term refers to women who meet the qualification of deacon. In a letter to the church in Cenchrea, Paul introduces Sister Phoebe as a servant of the church in reference to the specific office of women deacon or deaconess.

"I commend to you Phoebe our sister, who is a servant of the church in Cenchrea, that you may receive her in The Lord in a manner worthy of the saints, and assist her in whatever business she has need of you; for indeed she has been a helper of many and of myself also."

(Romans 16:1-2 NKJV)

There is no Bible reference that describes the duties of deacon and deaconess; they are truly servants of the church. Today's deacon fills an important role in the church, as assistant leaders in the ministry, preparing materials for taking of The Lord's Supper, assisting in baptism, care for the shut-in, serving the poor, and leading ministry groups.

The pastor, deacons, and deaconess meet monthly to plan and pray concerning the monthly events of the working church. The deacon and deaconess must have a clear understanding of faith and be a person of proven character.

The qualification of deacon and deaconess, including the conduct of their family, is clearly outlined.

"Likewise deacons must be reverent, not double-tongued, not given [addicted] to much wine, not greedy for money, holding the mystery of the faith with a pure conscience. But let these also first be tested; then let them serve as deacons, being found blameless. Likewise, their wives must be reverent, not slanderers, temperate, faithful in all things. Let deacons be the husbands of one wife, ruling their children and their own houses well. For those who have served well as deacons obtain for themselves a good standing and great boldness in the faith which is in Christ Jesus."
(1 Timothy 3:8-13 NKJV)

Other Officers

The duties of the administrative/clerical support department and the trustee department are defined by the church. The qualification for these officers are the same as the deacons (1 Timothy 3:8-13 NKJV).

These officers are elected by the church and are accountable to the church.

The Administrative/Clerical Support provides a full range of administrative and clerical support, scheduling appointments, creating and printing programs and maintain all church records.

"And God has appointed these in the church: first apostles, second prophets, third teachers, after

31

*that miracles, then gifts of healings, helps, adminis-
trations, varieties of tongues."*
(1Corinthians 12:28 NKJV)

The Trustee serves as steward over God's storehouse. The trustees hold legal title to all church property, and are responsible for its maintenance and upkeep. The trustees sign all documents relating to all purchases, sales, mortgages, and rent of church properties. The trustees maintain banking records and the disbursement of funds. They also maintain historical expenses and income data, analyze budget request of all ministries, produce profit and loss statements, and forecast the yearly church budget.

SERVICE MINISTRIES AND ORGANIZATIONS

A service organization or ministry is an activity that serves or assists others. In order to qualify as a ministry, the activity must align itself with one or more of the following duties:

Preaching the news of Jesus Christ

Governing/stewardship of the church

Teaching people

Encouraging people

Praying for people

Comforting people

Feeding people

Winning souls

Rebuking, and warning of apostasy.

A ministry must produce a mission statement that defines the task and its purpose, and is supported by Bible Scripture.

Example: the mission statement, to conduct Bible study for children ages six, seven, and eight at the time of the adult Wednesday Bible study is supported by

> *"Train up a child in the way he should go, and when he is old he will not depart from it."*
> **(Proverbs 22:6 NKJV)**

A ministry without a mission statement and Bible Scripture to support it is a "FAN CLUB." Most ministries require their members to sign a group covenant, a promise to work diligently, faithfully, and prayerfully toward the mission of that ministry. Each year, a board of ministers, deacons, and trustees reviews the ministry reports. These reports contain the previous year's accomplishments and the budget requirements. The board ensures there are no conflicts or duplication between ministries, and advises the ministry of any improvements needed to keep up God's work.

WORKING MINISTRY

Ushers Ministry are the doorkeepers in God's house, a ministry of hospitality and caring of the church.

> *"Berechiah and Elkanah were doorkeepers for the ark; Shebaniah, Joshaphat, Nethanel, Amasai, Zechariah, Benaiah, and Eliezer, the priests, were to blow the trumpets before the ark of God; and Obed-Edom and Jehiah, doorkeepers for the ark"*
> **(1Chronicles 15:23 24 NKJV)**

> *"Rejoicing in hope, patient in tribulation, continuing steadfastly in prayer; distributing to the needs of the saints, given to hospitality."*
> **(Romans 12:12-13 NKJV)**

There are times when members or newcomers come to church burdened, sad, and discouraged. They come expecting the Sunday services to be an experience of inspiration, and an uplifting renewed celebration. The usher, being the first person visible in the church, helps make that experience a reality for all by ensuring all see and experience his unconditional love.

Ushers greet the worshippers, making every attempt to help then feel welcome and at ease. They distribute bulletins, hymnals, and handouts, receive the tithes and offerings, and deliver them promptly to the Trustees.

> *"Go up to Hilkiah, the high priest, that he may count the money which has been brought into the house of The Lord, which the doorkeepers have gathered from the people."*
>
> **(2Kings 22:4 NKJV)**

Ushers maintain alertness for any emergency that may arise, contacting the proper persons to provide assistance, and directing worshippers out of the sanctuary in an orderly fashion.

The Ministry of Education provides guidance for Sunday schools, children's church, Bible study, and all training ministries.

The education ministry develops training programs to teach the doctrine, Christian ethics, Christian history, Church policy, and conducts workshops to certify teachers and improve Bible teaching methods.

> *"For whatever things were written before were written for our learning, that we through the patience and comfort of The Scriptures might have hope."*
>
> **(Romans 15:4 NKJV)**

Ministry of Music is probably the largest ministry of the church. Most churches have a youth choir, junior choir, adult choirs, women's choir, and all-male choirs. The music ministries provide voice training, musical training in piano, guitar, and drums for various age groups. Music ministries have succeeded in spreading the gospel to millions through music, by making tapes, CDs, radio and TV performances.

> *"Speaking to one another in psalms and hymns and spiritual songs, singing and making melody in your heart to The Lord."*
> **(Ephesians 5:19 NKJV)**

There are many other ministries and service organizations working in church government and operation and those working inside and outside the church spreading the gospel and enlisting new believers. To name just a few:

Family Counseling/Marriage Enrichment

Food Services

New Members Orientation

Tutoring, Youth

Transportation

Prison Ministry

You may have encountered that church worker who is an usher, choir member, a trustee and chairperson of another ministry. Most likely, this person truly wants only to serve God and the church in any and all ways possible. It is not impossible, but highly unlikely that one person can serve effectively and efficiently in all positions.

In the book of Romans, Paul writes, "we all have different gifts."

> *"Having then gifts differing according to the grace that is given to us, let us use them: if prophecy, let us prophesy in proportion to our faith; or ministry, let us use it in our ministering; he who teaches,*

in teaching; he who exhorts, in exhortation; he who gives, with liberality; he who leads, with diligence; he who shows mercy, with cheerfulness."
(Romans 12:6-8 NKJV)

Your gifts may be working in a service ministry outside the church. There are so many to consider. As a Christian, the way we live our lives, our behavior, our attitude toward one another, may be considered a ministry. Many times, it only takes one act of kindness or just one word to start spreading the gospel and enlisting new believers.

WHAT'S "AH"?

(Dictionary)

From age five to seven, my granddaughter was always asking, "Grandpa, what is that?" Or "Why is that?" The older she became, the question became shortened to "What's ah this?" and "What's ah pulpit?" Therefore, this chapter is titled

"What's Ah?"

As we Christians fellowship with one another, we learn many words and expressions that we accept without knowing where they come from or why. For instance, the word "Fellowship" We all know what it means basically, but why is it used most commonly among Christians?

The word *fellowship* is a translation of the Hebrew stem hor, and the Greek stem Koin, which was used to express ideas such as a common or shared house, the binding or joining.

An important part of Hebrew life was sharing together in the study of Scripture and law and the fellowship table (common table).

FELLOWSHIP: the bond of common purpose and devotion that binds Christians together and to Christ.

What's AH?

Amen:

Hebrew translation of a word that expresses approval, truly, certainly, so be it. Affirms what has been said or prayed.

Amen corner:

The seats to the minister's right, occupied by those leading the responsive "amen" in rural Protestant churches.

Apostasy:

Falling away from God's truth, the abandoning of what one has believed in as a faith.

Apostles; Disciples:

Apostles: The Greek term [apostolos] which means a messenger sent out on a special mission on behalf of others. (The twelve disciples sent out by Christ to teach the gospel).

Disciple: The Greek word meaning "learn" or "pupil."

It was the duty of the disciple to learn, study, and pass along the teaching of the master.

Blaspheme:

"To speak harm." Speaking carelessly, falsely, or insultingly about God or Holy things. (Mark 3:29 NKJV)

Born Again:

Refers to the experience of salvation; entering God's family through faith in Christ. (John 3:3; 1Peter 1:23 NKJV)

Brother; Sister:

Title used by the Christian community to express a spiritual relationship. (Luke 8:20-21; Matthew 12:49- 50 NKJV]

Bishop:

The Greek term [episkopos) meant inspector, watchman, or overseer. Before Christianity, the term referred to finance officers who administered revenues for the Greek temples. Today, churches have one bishop as overseer of nearby rural churches as well as the city church. Qualifications, see 1 Timothy 3:1; Titus 1:7 NKJV.

Christ:

Official title of Jesus, in the Greek term (christos) meaning "anointed." The Hebrew term (mashiach) meaning the "anointed one" -messiah. (Matthew1:16 NKJV)

Christian:

One committed to Christ , a follower of Christ . The disciples were called Christians first at Antioch. The word Christian is used three times in The Bible : Acts 11:26,
Acts 26:28, and 1Peter 4:16.

Church:

The entire group of people who believe in Jesus. (1Corinthians 12:12-31 NKJV)

Communion:

The term used by the Church to refer to their celebration of Jesus' final memorial supper with His disciples.

Covenant:

A pact: alliance: or agreement between two parties of equal or unequal authority. For example: God's covenant with Noah. (Genesis 9:8-9; Exodus 19:5 NKJV)

Deacon and deaconess:

A translation of the Greek word "DIAKONOS" which means servant or minister. For qualifications, see (1Timothy 3:8-13 NKJV.)

Elder:

Older men of the tribe were the leaders of the community and made all important decisions. Now they are leaders in the Church. (Exodus 3:16-18; 1 Timothy 5:17;Titus 1:5 NKJV)

Fellowship:

The bond of common purpose and devotion that bonds Christians together with Christ . (1John 1:3, 1:6-7 NKJV)

Hallelujah:

Praise The Lord, a song of praise. [Revelation 19:1 NKJV)

Pastor:

A man called by God to preach the gospel and serve as church leader and overseer. (Jeremiah 3:15 NKJV)

Pentecost:

One of three major Jewish festivals: (Passover, Feast of Tabernacles and Pentecost). Also known as the "The feast of weeks" The festival at which The Holy Spirit came on early church. (Acts 2;1, Acts 20:16)

Prophet:

One called to speak a word from The Lord through direct prompting of The Holy Spirit . (Exodus 7:1 NKJV)

Pulpit:

An elevated platform which a speaker stood, not a lectern or high reading desk behind which a leader stands. (Nehemiah 8:4 NKJV)

Scripture:

"A writing"; renderings; the Latin *scriptura* and the Greek *graphe*. The term is used fifty times in The New Testament (Acts 17:11). We now have a completed Scripture consisting of The Old and New Testament.

> *"That Christ may dwell in your hearts through faith; that you, being rooted and grounded in love, may be able to comprehend with all the saints what is the width and length and depth and height."*
>
> Ephesians 3:17-18, NKJV

THE OPEN PLAN

Read The Bible in one year

The Old Testament book of Nehemiah tell us how The Bible (the book of law) was read to an assembly of men and women and all who were able to understand. (Nehemiah 8:1-6)

During that time, there were very few Bibles in print; today, The Bible is available to all who are able to understand. The Bible has been translated into more than290 languages and dialects, and more than 30 million copies are sold each year. How many of us have actually read The Bible cover-to-cover?

Reading The Bible cover-to-cover can be a monumental task for many. The Bible's length is like reading a small library; it contains sixty-six books written by dozens of authors, from all walks of life, from kings to shepherds. Others rely on Bible study classes and the pastor's sermon for Bible reading.

The new believers can think of reading The Bible cover-to-cover as reading a mystery, "You may not understand the entire clues in the beginning, but at the end, you will say, "Oh yes, I get it now."

As you read The Bible , you will come to understand that The Bible is more than just a guidebook of life; God's Word guarantees our future forever.

The open plan combines reading The Bible cover to cover with Bible study. Read just fifteen minutes a day every day, then on the seventh day, summarize your insights of the past seven days' reading and write down a verse you want to remember.

The open plan is only a tool that keeps us focus on the goal, the goal of reading and studying The Bible . The only requirement is to read every day. It is not difficult to find fifteen minutes each day; in fact, most days we have more than fifteen minutes' free time a day. Some are able to read the complete Bible in eight months, others in eighteen months.

Although it is not a requirement, using a study Bible, and a Bible dictionary will be very helpful. Most study Bibles offer many outstanding features, such as:

Study notes,

Book introduction and outlines Cross-references,

Parallel passages between people and events, maps,

Timelines

A concordance and more

A Bible dictionary shows you how to pronounce a word or name and its meaning and biblical usage.

The goal is reading and studying The Bible daily. The open plan allows you to start from the beginning on any month and day you choose, but you must choose.

Month _____

Day_____	Genesis 1:1 – Genesis 3:24
Day_____	Genesis 4:1 – Genesis 6:22
Day_____	Genesis 7:1 – Genesis 9:28
Day_____	Genesis 10:1 – Genesis 12:20
Day_____	Genesis 13:1 – Genesis 15:24
Day_____	Genesis 16:1 – Genesis 18:33
Day_____	Genesis 19:1 – Genesis 21:34

Open Plan

Reading time 15 minutes each day

Old Testament.

Summarize the past seven day's evening:

_____

_____

_____

_____

A verse you would like to remember:

_____

_____

_____

_____

Month _____

Day_____ Genesis 22:1 – Genesis 24:67

Day_____ Genesis 25:1 – Genesis 27:46

Day_____ Genesis 28:1 – Genesis 30:43

Day_____ Genesis 31:1 – Genesis 33:19

Day_____ Genesis 34:1 – Genesis 36:40

Day_____ Genesis 37:1 – Genesis 39:23

Day_____ Genesis 40:1 – Genesis 42:38

Open Plan

Reading time 15 minutes each day

Old Testament.

Summarize the past seven day's evening:

_____
_____
_____
_____

A verse you would like to remember:

_____
_____
_____
_____

Month _____

Day_____	Genesis 43:1 – Genesis 45:28
Day_____	Genesis 46:1 – Genesis 48:22
Day_____	Genesis 49:1 – Exodus 1:22
Day_____	Exodus 2:1 – Exodus 4:31
Day_____	Exodus 5:1 – Exodus 7:24
Day_____	Exodus 8:1 – Exodus 10:35
Day_____	Exodus 11:1 – Exodus 13:10

Open Plan

Reading time 15 minutes each day

Old Testament.

Summarize the past seven day's evening:

_____
_____
_____
_____

A verse you would like to remember:

_____
_____
_____
_____

Month _____

Day_____	Exodus 14:1 – Exodus 16:36
Day_____	Exodus 17:1 – Exodus 19:25
Day_____	Exodus 20:1 – Exodus 22:31
Day_____	Exodus 23:1 – Exodus 25:40
Day_____	Exodus 26:1 – Exodus 28:43
Day_____	Exodus 29:1 – Exodus 31:18
Day_____	Exodus 32:1 – Exodus 34:35

Open Plan

Reading time 15 minutes each day

Old Testament.

Summarize the past seven day's evening:

_____
_____
_____
_____

A verse you would like to remember:

_____
_____
_____
_____

Month _____

Day_____	Exodus 35:1 – Exodus 37:29
Day_____	Exodus 38:1 – Exodus 39:42
Day_____	Exodus 40:1 – Exodus 40:38
Day_____	Leviticus 1:1 – Leviticus 3:17
Day_____	Leviticus 4:1 – Leviticus 6:30
Day_____	Leviticus 7:1 – Leviticus 8:38
Day_____	Leviticus 9:1 – Leviticus 10:20

Open Plan

Reading time 15 minutes each day

Old Testament.

Summarize the past seven day's evening:

_____
_____
_____
_____

A verse you would like to remember:

_____
_____
_____

Month _____

Day_____	Leviticus 11:1 – Leviticus 13:59
Day_____	Leviticus 14:1 – Leviticus 15:33
Day_____	Leviticus 16:1 – Leviticus 18:30
Day_____	Leviticus 19:1 – Leviticus 21:24
Day_____	Leviticus 22:1 – Leviticus 23:33
Day_____	Leviticus 24:1 – Leviticus 25:54
Day_____	Leviticus 26:1 – Leviticus 27:34

Open Plan

Reading time 15 minutes each day

Old Testament.

Summarize the past seven day's evening:

_____
_____
_____
_____

A verse you would like to remember:

_____
_____
_____
_____

Month _____

Day_____	Numbers 1:1 – Numbers 2:34
Day_____	Numbers 3:1 – Numbers 4:49
Day_____	Numbers 5:1 – Numbers 6:27
Day_____	Numbers 7:1 – Numbers 7:89
Day_____	Numbers 8:1 – Numbers 9:23
Day_____	Numbers 10:1 – Numbers 11:35
Day_____	Numbers 12:1 – Numbers 13:33

Open Plan

Reading time 15 minutes each day

Old Testament.

Summarize the past seven day's evening:

_____

_____

_____

_____

A verse you would like to remember:

_____

_____

_____

_____

Month _____

Day_____	Numbers 14:1 – Numbers 15:41
Day_____	Numbers 16:1 – Numbers 18:32
Day_____	Numbers 19:1 – Numbers 20:29
Day_____	Numbers 21:1 – Numbers 22:41
Day_____	Numbers 23:1 – Numbers 25:17
Day_____	Numbers 26:1 – Numbers 27:23
Day_____	Numbers 28:1 – Numbers 29:40

Open Plan

Reading time 15 minutes each day

Old Testament.

Summarize the past seven day's evening:

_____
_____
_____
_____

A verse you would like to remember:

_____
_____
_____
_____

Month _____

Day_____	Deuteronomy 11:1 – Deuteronomy 13:18
Day_____	Deuteronomy 14:1 – Deuteronomy 16:22
Day_____	Deuteronomy 17:1 – Deuteronomy 20:20
Day_____	Deuteronomy 21:1 – Deuteronomy 23:25
Day_____	Deuteronomy 24:1 – Deuteronomy 27:26
Day_____	Deuteronomy 28:1 – Deuteronomy 28:20
Day_____	Deuteronomy 29:1 – Deuteronomy 31:30

Open Plan

Reading time 15 minutes each day

Old Testament.

Summarize the past seven day's evening:

_____

_____

_____

_____

A verse you would like to remember:

_____

_____

_____

_____

Month _____

Day_____	Deuteronomy 32:1 – Deuteronomy 34:12
Day_____	Joshua 1:1 – Joshua 3:17
Day_____	Joshua 4:1 – Joshua 6:27
Day_____	Joshua 7:1 – Joshua 8:35
Day_____	Joshua 9:1 – Joshua 10:43
Day_____	Joshua 11:1 – Joshua 13:33
Day_____	Joshua 14:1 – Joshua 16:10

Open Plan

Reading time 15 minutes each day

Old Testament.

Summarize the past seven day's evening:

_____
_____
_____
_____

A verse you would like to remember:

_____
_____
_____
_____

Month _____

Day_____	Joshua 17:1 – Joshua 19:51
Day_____	Joshua 20:1 – Joshua 21:45
Day_____	Joshua 22:1 – Joshua 24:33
Day_____	Judges 1:1 – Judges 2:23
Day_____	Judges 3:1 – Judges 5:31
Day_____	Judges 6:1 – Judges 7:25
Day_____	Judges 8:1 – Judges 9:57

<u>Open Plan</u>

Reading time 15 minutes each day

<u>Old Testament.</u>

Summarize the past seven day's evening:

_____
_____
_____
_____

A verse you would like to remember:

_____
_____
_____
_____

Month _____

Day_____	Judges 10:1 – Judges 11:39
Day_____	Judges 12:1 – Judges 14:29
Day_____	Judges 15:1 – Judges 17:13
Day_____	Judges 18:1 – Judges 19:30
Day_____	Judges 20:1 – Judges 21:25
Day_____	Ruth 1:1 – Ruth 4:22
Day_____	1Samuel 1:1 – 1Samuel 3:21

Open Plan

Reading time 15 minutes each day

Old Testament.

Summarize the past seven day's evening:

_____
_____
_____
_____

A verse you would like to remember:

_____
_____
_____
_____

Month _____

Day_____	1Samuel 4:1 – 1Samuel 7:17
Day_____	1Samuel 8:1 – 1Samuel 11:15
Day_____	1Samuel 12:1 – 1Samuel 14:23
Day_____	1Samuel 14:24 – 1Samuel 16:23
Day_____	1Samuel 17:1 – 1Samuel 18:30
Day_____	1Samuel 19:1 – 1Samuel 21:15
Day_____	1Samuel 22:1 – 1Samuel 24:22

Open Plan

Reading time 15 minutes each day

Old Testament.

Summarize the past seven day's evening:

_____
_____
_____
_____

A verse you would like to remember:

_____
_____
_____
_____

Month _____

Day_____	1Samuel 25:1 – 1Samuel 27:12
Day_____	1Samuel 28:1 – 1Samuel 31:13
Day_____	2Samuel 1:1 – 2Samuel 2:32
Day_____	2Samuel 3:1 – 2Samuel 5:25
Day_____	2Samuel 6:1 – 2Samuel 9:13
Day_____	2Samuel 10:1 – 2Samuel 12:31
Day_____	2Samuel 13:1 – 2Samuel 14:33

Open Plan

Reading time 15 minutes each day

Old Testament.

Summarize the past seven day's evening:

_____
_____
_____
_____

A verse you would like to remember:

_____
_____
_____
_____

Month _____

Day_____ 2Samuel 15:1 – 2Samuel 16:23

Day_____ 2Samuel 17:1 – 2Samuel 18:33

Day_____ 2Samuel 19:1 – 2Samuel 20:26

Day_____ 2Samuel 21:1 – 2Samuel 22:51

Day_____ 2Samuel 23:1 – 2Samuel 24:25

Day_____ 1Kings 1:1 – 1Kings 2:25

Day_____ 1Kings 2:26 – 1Kings 4:34

Open Plan

Reading time 15 minutes each day

Old Testament.

Summarize the past seven day's evening:

_____

_____

_____

_____

A verse you would like to remember:

_____

_____

_____

_____

Month _____

Day_____	1Kings 5:1 – 1Kings 7:51
Day_____	1Kings 8:1 – 1Kings 8:66
Day_____	1Kings 9:1 – 1Kings 11:43
Day_____	1Kings 12:1 – 1Kings 13:34
Day_____	1Kings 14:1 – 1Kings 15:34
Day_____	1Kings 16:1 – 1Kings 18:46
Day_____	1Kings 19:1 – 1Kings 20:43

Open Plan

Reading time 15 minutes each day

Old Testament.

Summarize the past seven day's evening:

_____
_____
_____
_____

A verse you would like to remember:

_____
_____
_____
_____

Month _____

Day_____	1Kings 21:1 – 1Kings 22:53
Day_____	2Kings 1:1 – 2Kings 3:27
Day_____	2Kings 4:1 – 2Kings 5:27
Day_____	2Kings 6:6 – 2Kings 8:29
Day_____	2Kings 9:1 – 2Kings 10:21
Day_____	2Kings 11:1 – 2Kings 23:25
Day_____	2Kings 14:1 – 2Kings 15:38

Open Plan

Reading time 15 minutes each day

Old Testament.

Summarize the past seven day's evening:

_____
_____
_____
_____

A verse you would like to remember:

_____
_____
_____
_____

Month _____

Day_____	2Kings 16:1 – 1Kings 17:41
Day_____	2Kings 18:1 – 2Kings 20:21
Day_____	2Kings 21:1 – 2Kings 23:20
Day_____	2Kings 23:21 – 2Kings 25:30
Day_____	1Chronicles 1:1 – 1Chronicles 2:54
Day_____	1Chronicles 3:1 – 1Chronicles 5:26
Day_____	1Chronicles 6:1 – 1Chronicles 7:40

Open Plan

Reading time 15 minutes each day

Old Testament.

Summarize the past seven day's evening:

_____
_____
_____
_____

A verse you would like to remember:

_____
_____
_____
_____

Month _____

Day_____	1Chronicles 8:1 – 1Chronicles 10:14
Day_____	1Chronicles 11:1 – 1Chronicles 13:14
Day_____	1Chronicles 14:1 – 1Chronicles 16:43
Day_____	1Chronicles 17:1 – 1Chronicles 20:8
Day_____	1Chronicles 21:1 – 1Chronicles 23:32
Day_____	1Chronicles 24:1 – 1Chronicles 26:32
Day_____	1Chronicles 27:1 – 1Chronicles 29:30

Open Plan

Reading time 15 minutes each day

Old Testament.

Summarize the past seven day's evening:

_____
_____
_____
_____

A verse you would like to remember:

_____
_____
_____
_____

Month _____

Day_____	2Chronicles 1:1 – 2Chronicles 3:17
Day_____	2Chronicles 4:1 – 2Chronicles 6:42
Day_____	2Chronicles 7:1 – 2Chronicles 9:30
Day_____	2Chronicles 10:1 – 2Chronicles 13:22
Day_____	2Chronicles 14:1 – 2Chronicles 17:19
Day_____	2Chronicles 18:1 – 2Chronicles 20:37
Day_____	2Chronicles 21:1 – 2Chronicles 24:27

Open Plan

Reading time 15 minutes each day

Old Testament.

Summarize the past seven day's evening:

_____
_____
_____
_____

A verse you would like to remember:

_____
_____
_____
_____

Month _____

Day_____	2Chronicles 25:1 – 2Chronicles 27:9
Day_____	2Chronicles 28:1 – 2Chronicles 30:27
Day_____	2Chronicles 31:1 – 2Chronicles 33:25
Day_____	2Chronicles 34:1 – 2Chronicles 36:23
Day_____	Ezra 1:1 – Ezra 2:70
Day_____	Ezra 3:1 – Ezra 5:17
Day_____	Ezra 6:1 – Ezra 7:28

Open Plan

Reading time 15 minutes each day

Old Testament.

Summarize the past seven day's evening:

_____

_____

_____

_____

A verse you would like to remember:

_____

_____

_____

_____

Month _____

Day_____	Ezra 3:1 – Ezra 5:17
Day_____	Ezra 6:1 – Ezra 7:28
Day_____	Nehemiah 1:1 – Nehemiah 3:32
Day_____	Nehemiah 4:1 – Nehemiah 6:19
Day_____	Nehemiah 7:1 – Nehemiah 8:18
Day_____	Nehemiah 9:1 – Nehemiah 10:39
Day_____	Nehemiah 11:1 – Nehemiah 12:47

Open Plan

Reading time 15 minutes each day

Old Testament.

Summarize the past seven day's evening:

_____
_____
_____
_____

A verse you would like to remember:

_____
_____
_____
_____

Month _____

Day_____	Nehemiah 13:1 – Nehemiah 13:30
Day_____	Esther 1:1 – Esther 3:15
Day_____	Esther 4:1 – Esther 7:10
Day_____	Esther 8:1 – Esther 10:3
Day_____	Job 1:1 – Job 4:21
Day_____	Job 5:1 – Job 8:22
Day_____	Job 9:1 – Job 12:25

Open Plan

Reading time 15 minutes each day

Old Testament.

Summarize the past seven day's evening:

_____

_____

_____

_____

A verse you would like to remember:

_____

_____

_____

_____

Month _____

Day_____	Job 13:1 – Job 16:22
Day_____	Job 17:1 – Job 20:29
Day_____	Job 21:1 – Job 24:24
Day_____	Job 25:1 – Job 59:25
Day_____	Job 30:1 – Job 33:33
Day_____	Job 34:1 – Job 37:24
Day_____	Job 38:1 – Job 40:24

<u>Open Plan</u>

Reading time 15 minutes each day

<u>Old Testament.</u>

Summarize the past seven day's evening:

_____

_____

_____

_____

A verse you would like to remember:

_____

_____

_____

_____

Month _____

Day_____	Job 41:1 – Job 42:24
Day_____	Psalm 1:1 – Psalm 9:20
Day_____	Psalm 10:1 – Psalm 17:15
Day_____	Psalm 18:1 – Psalm 22:31
Day_____	Psalm 23:1 – Psalm 30:12
Day_____	Psalm 31:1 – Psalm 35:28
Day_____	Psalm 36:1 – Psalm 39:13

<u>Open Plan</u>

Reading time 15 minutes each day

<u>Old Testament.</u>

Summarize the past seven day's evening:

_____
_____
_____
_____

A verse you would like to remember:

_____
_____
_____
_____

Month _____

Day_____	Psalm 40:1 – Psalm 45:17
Day_____	Psalm 46:1 – Psalm 51:19
Day_____	Psalm 52:1 – Psalm 59:17
Day_____	Psalm 60:1 – Psalm 66:20
Day_____	Psalm 67:1 – Psalm 71:24
Day_____	Psalm 72:1 – Psalm 77:20
Day_____	Psalm 78:1 – Psalm 80:19

Open Plan

Reading time 15 minutes each day

Old Testament.

Summarize the past seven day's evening:

_____
_____
_____
_____

A verse you would like to remember:

_____
_____
_____
_____

Month _____

Day_____	Psalm 81:1 – Psalm 87:7
Day_____	Psalm 88:1 – Psalm 91:16
Day_____	Psalm 92:1 – Psalm 100:5
Day_____	Psalm 101:1 – Psalm 105:45
Day_____	Psalm 106:1 – Psalm 107:43
Day_____	Psalm 108:1 – Psalm 118:29
Day_____	Psalm 119:1 – Psalm 119:176

Open Plan

Reading time 15 minutes each day

Old Testament.

Summarize the past seven day's evening:

_____
_____
_____
_____

A verse you would like to remember:

_____
_____
_____
_____

Month _____

Day_____	Psalm 120:1 – Psalm 131:3
Day_____	Psalm 132:1 – Psalm 138:8
Day_____	Psalm 139:1 – Psalm 143:12
Day_____	Psalm 144:1 – Psalm 150:6
Day_____	Proverbs 1:1 – Proverbs 3:35
Day_____	Proverbs 4:1 – Proverbs 7:27
Day_____	Proverbs 8:1 – Proverbs 11:31

Open Plan

Reading time 15 minutes each day

Old Testament.

Summarize the past seven day's evening:

_____
_____
_____
_____

A verse you would like to remember:

_____
_____
_____
_____

Month _____

Day_____ Proverbs 12:1 – Proverbs 15:33

Day_____ Proverbs 16:1 – Proverbs 19:29

Day_____ Proverbs 20:1 – Proverbs 22:29

Day_____ Proverbs 23:1 – Proverbs 26:28

Day_____ Proverbs 27:1 – Proverbs 31:31

Day_____ Ecclesiastes 1:1 – Ecclesiastes 4:16

Day_____ Ecclesiastes 5:1 – Ecclesiastes 8:17

<u>Open Plan</u>

Reading time 15 minutes each day

<u>Old Testament.</u>

Summarize the past seven day's evening:

_____

_____

_____

_____

A verse you would like to remember:

_____

_____

_____

_____

Month _____

Day_____	Ecclesiastes 9:1 – Ecclesiastes 12:14
Day_____	Song of Solomon 1:1 – Song of Solomon 8:14
Day_____	Isaiah 1:1 – Isaiah 4:6
Day_____	Isaiah 5:1 – Isaiah 9:21
Day_____	Isaiah 10:1 – Isaiah 14:32
Day_____	Isaiah 15:1 – Isaiah 21:17
Day_____	Isaiah 22:1 – Isaiah 26:21

Open Plan

Reading time 15 minutes each day

Old Testament.

Summarize the past seven day's evening:

_____
_____
_____
_____

A verse you would like to remember:

_____
_____
_____
_____

Month _____

Day_____	Isaiah 27:1 – Isaiah 31:9
Day_____	Isaiah 32:1 – Isaiah 37:38
Day_____	Isaiah 38:1 – Isaiah 42:25
Day_____	Isaiah 43:1 – Isaiah 46:23
Day_____	Isaiah 47:1 – Isaiah 51:23
Day_____	Isaiah 52:1 – Isaiah 57:21
Day_____	Isaiah 58:1 – Isaiah 63:19

Open Plan

Reading time 15 minutes each day

Old Testament.

Summarize the past seven day's evening:

_____
_____
_____
_____

A verse you would like to remember:

_____
_____
_____
_____

Month _____

Day_____	Isaiah 64:1 – Isaiah 66:24
Day_____	Jeremiah 1:1 – Jeremiah 3:25
Day_____	Jeremiah 4:1 – Jeremiah 6:30
Day_____	Jeremiah 7:1 – Jeremiah 10:25
Day_____	Jeremiah 11:1 – Jeremiah 14:22
Day_____	Jeremiah 15:1 – Jeremiah 18:23
Day_____	Jeremiah 19:1 – Jeremiah 22:38

Open Plan

Reading time 15 minutes each day

Old Testament.

Summarize the past seven day's evening:

_____
_____
_____
_____

A verse you would like to remember:

_____
_____
_____
_____

Month _____

Day_____ Jeremiah 23:1 – Jeremiah 25:38

Day_____ Jeremiah 26:1 – Jeremiah 28:17

Day_____ Jeremiah 29:1 – Jeremiah 31:40

Day_____ Jeremiah 32:1 – Jeremiah 33:26

Day_____ Jeremiah 34:1 – Jeremiah 36:32

Day_____ Jeremiah 37:1 – Jeremiah 40:16

Day_____ Jeremiah 41:1 – Jeremiah 44:30

Open Plan

Reading time 15 minutes each day

Old Testament.

Summarize the past seven day's evening:

_____

_____

_____

_____

A verse you would like to remember:

_____

_____

_____

_____

Month _____

Day_____	Jeremiah 45:1 – Jeremiah 48:47
Day_____	Jeremiah 49:1 – Jeremiah 50:46
Day_____	Jeremiah 51:1 – Jeremiah 52:34
Day_____	Lamentations 1:1 – Lamentations 2:22
Day_____	Lamentations 3:1 – Lamentations 5:22
Day_____	Ezekiel 1:1 – Ezekiel 4:17
Day_____	Ezekiel 5:1 – Ezekiel 9:11

Open Plan

Reading time 15 minutes each day

Old Testament.

Summarize the past seven day's evening:

_____
_____
_____
_____

A verse you would like to remember:

_____
_____
_____
_____

Month _____

Day_____	Ezekiel 10:1 – Ezekiel 13:23
Day_____	Ezekiel 14:1 – Ezekiel 16:63
Day_____	Ezekiel 17:1 – Ezekiel 19:14
Day_____	Ezekiel 20:1 – Ezekiel 21:32
Day_____	Ezekiel 22:1 – Ezekiel 24:27
Day_____	Ezekiel 25:1 – Ezekiel 28:26
Day_____	Ezekiel 29:1 – Ezekiel 32:32

Open Plan

Reading time 15 minutes each day

Old Testament.

Summarize the past seven day's evening:

_____
_____
_____
_____

A verse you would like to remember:

_____
_____
_____
_____

Month _____

Day_____	Ezekiel 33:1 – Ezekiel 36:38
Day_____	Ezekiel 37:1 – Ezekiel 39:29
Day_____	Ezekiel 40:1 – Ezekiel 42:20
Day_____	Ezekiel 43:1 – Ezekiel 45:25
Day_____	Ezekiel 46:1 – Ezekiel 48:35
Day_____	Daniel 1:1 – Daniel 3:30
Day_____	Daniel 4:1 – Daniel 6:28

Open Plan

Reading time 15 minutes each day

Old Testament.

Summarize the past seven day's evening:

_____
_____
_____
_____

A verse you would like to remember:

_____
_____
_____
_____

Month _____

Day_____	Daniel 7:1 – Daniel 9:27
Day_____	Daniel 10:1 – Daniel 12:13
Day_____	Hosea 1:1 – Hosea 6:11
Day_____	Hosea 7:1 – Hosea 14:9
Day_____	Joel 1:1 – Joel 3:21
Day_____	Amos 1:1 – Amos 5:27
Day_____	Amos 6:1 – Obadiah 1:21

Open Plan

Reading time 15 minutes each day

Old Testament.

Summarize the past seven day's evening:

_____
_____
_____
_____

A verse you would like to remember:

_____
_____
_____
_____

Month _____

Day_____	Jonah 1:1 – Jonah 4:11
Day_____	Micah 1:1 – Micah 7:20
Day_____	Nahum 1:1 – Habbakkuk 3:19
Day_____	Zephaniah 1:1 – Haggai 3:23
Day_____	Zechariah 1:1 – Zechariah 7:14
Day_____	Zechariah 8:1 – Zechariah 14:21
Day_____	Malachi 1:1 – Malachi 4:6

Open Plan

Reading time 15 minutes each day

Old Testament.

Summarize the past seven day's evening:

_____
_____
_____
_____

A verse you would like to remember:

_____
_____
_____
_____

Month _____

Day_____	Matthew 1:1 – Matthew 3:17
Day_____	Matthew 4:1 – Matthew 6:34
Day_____	Matthew 7:1 – Matthew 9:38
Day_____	Matthew 10:1 – Matthew 11:30
Day_____	Matthew 12:1 – Matthew 12:50
Day_____	Matthew 13:1 – Matthew 14:36
Day_____	Matthew 15:1 – Matthew 17:27

Open Plan

Reading time 15 minutes each day

Old Testament.

Summarize the past seven day's evening:

_____
_____
_____
_____

A verse you would like to remember:

_____
_____
_____
_____

Month _____

Day_____   Matthew 18:1 – Matthew 20:34

Day_____   Matthew 21:1 – Matthew 22:44

Day_____   Matthew 23:1 – Matthew 24:51

Day_____   Matthew 25:1 – Matthew 26:75

Day_____   Matthew 27:1 – Matthew 28:20

Day_____   Mark 13:1 – Mark 14:36

Day_____   Mark 15:1 – Mark 17:27

Open Plan

Reading time 15 minutes each day

Old Testament.

Summarize the past seven day's evening:

_____
_____
_____
_____

A verse you would like to remember:

_____
_____
_____
_____

Month _____

Day_____	Mark 6:1 – Mark 7:37
Day_____	Mark 8:1 – Mark 9:50
Day_____	Mark 10:1 – Mark 11:33
Day_____	Mark 12:1 – Mark 13:37
Day_____	Mark 14:1 – Mark 16:20
Day_____	Luke 1:1 – Luke 1:80
Day_____	Luke 2:1 – Luke 3:38

Open Plan

Reading time 15 minutes each day

Old Testament.

Summarize the past seven day's evening:

_____

_____

_____

_____

A verse you would like to remember:

_____

_____

_____

_____

Month _____

Open Plan

Reading time 15 minutes each day

Old Testament.

Summarize the past seven day's evening:

_____
_____
_____
_____

A verse you would like to remember:

_____
_____
_____
_____

Month _____

Day_____	Luke 19:1 – Luke 20:39
Day_____	Luke 21:1 – Luke 22:50
Day_____	Luke 23 – Luke 24:62
Day_____	John 1:1 – John 3:54
Day_____	John 4:1 – John 5:54
Day_____	John 6:1 – John 8:54
Day_____	John 9:1 – John 10:54

Open Plan

Reading time 15 minutes each day

Old Testament.

Summarize the past seven day's evening:

_____

_____

_____

_____

A verse you would like to remember:

_____

_____

_____

_____

Month _____

Day_____ John 11:1 – John 12:50

Day_____ John 13:1 – John 16:33

Day_____ John 17:1 – John 18:40

Day_____ John 19:1 – John 21:25

Day_____ Acts 1:1 – Acts 3:26

Day_____ Acts 4:1 – Acts 6:15

Day_____ Acts 7:1 – Acts 8:40

Open Plan

Reading time 15 minutes each day

Old Testament.

Summarize the past seven day's evening:

_____

_____

_____

_____

A verse you would like to remember:

_____

_____

_____

_____

Month _____

Day_____	Acts 9:1 – Acts 10:48
Day_____	Acts 11:1 – Acts 13:52
Day_____	Acts 14:1 – Acts 16:40
Day_____	Acts 17:1 – Acts 19:41
Day_____	Acts 20:1 – Acts 22:30
Day_____	Acts 23:1 – Acts 25:27
Day_____	Acts 26:1 – Acts 28:31

Open Plan

Reading time 15 minutes each day

Old Testament.

Summarize the past seven day's evening:

_____
_____
_____
_____

A verse you would like to remember:

_____
_____
_____
_____

Month _____

Day_____	Romans 1:1 – Romans 3:31
Day_____	Romans 4:1 – Romans 7:25
Day_____	Romans 8:1 – Romans 10:21
Day_____	Romans 11:1 – Romans 10:48
Day_____	Romans 9:1 – Romans 10:48
Day_____	1Corinthians 23:1 – 1Corinthians 25:27
Day_____	1Corinthians 23:1 – 1Corinthians 25:27

Open Plan

Reading time 15 minutes each day

Old Testament.

Summarize the past seven day's evening:

_____
_____
_____
_____

A verse you would like to remember:

_____
_____
_____
_____

Month _____

Day_____	1Corinthians 10:1 – 1Corinthians 13:13
Day_____	1Corinthians 14:1 – 1Corinthians 16:24
Day_____	2Corinthians 1:1 – 2Corinthians 4:18
Day_____	2Corinthians 5:1 – 2Corinthians 8:24
Day_____	2Corinthians 9:1 – 2Corinthians 13:14
Day_____	Galatians 1:1 – Galatians 3:29
Day_____	Galatians 4:1 – Galatians 6:18

Open Plan

Reading time 15 minutes each day

Old Testament.

Summarize the past seven day's evening:

_____
_____
_____
_____

A verse you would like to remember:

_____
_____
_____
_____

Month _____

Day_____	1Corinthians 10:1 – 1Corinthians 13:13
Day_____	1Corinthians 14:1 – 1Corinthians 16:24
Day_____	2Corinthians 1:1 – 2Corinthians 4:18
Day_____	2Corinthians 5:1 – 2Corinthians 8:24
Day_____	2Corinthians 9:1 – 2Corinthians 13:14
Day_____	Galatians 1:1 – Galatians 3:29
Day_____	Galatians 4:1 – Galatians 6:18

Open Plan

Reading time 15 minutes each day

Old Testament.

Summarize the past seven day's evening:

_____

_____

_____

_____

A verse you would like to remember:

_____

_____

_____

_____

Month _____

Day_____	Ephesians 1:1 – Ephesians 3:21
Day_____	Ephesians 4:1 – Ephesians 6:24
Day_____	Philippians 1:1 – Philippians 4:23
Day_____	Colossians 1:1 – Colossians 4:18
Day_____	1Thessalonians 1:1 – 1Thessalonians 5:28
Day_____	2Thessalonians 1:1 – 2Thessalonians 3:18
Day_____	1Timothy 1:1 – 1Timothy 6:21

Open Plan

Reading time 15 minutes each day

Old Testament.

Summarize the past seven day's evening:

_____

_____

_____

_____

A verse you would like to remember:

_____

_____

_____

_____

Month _____

Open Plan

Reading time 15 minutes each day

Old Testament.

Summarize the past seven day's evening:

_____
_____
_____
_____

A verse you would like to remember:

_____
_____
_____
_____

Month _____

Day_____	1Peter 1:1 – 1Peter 2:25
Day_____	1Peter 3:1 – 1Peter 5:14
Day_____	2Peter 1:1 – 2Peter 3:18
Day_____	1John 1:1 – 1John 3:24
Day_____	1John 4:1 – 1John 5:21
Day_____	2John 1:1 – Jude 1:25
Day_____	Revelation 1:1 – Revelation 2:29

Open Plan

Reading time 15 minutes each day

Old Testament.

Summarize the past seven day's evening:

_____

_____

_____

_____

A verse you would like to remember:

_____

_____

_____

_____

Month _____

Day_____ Revelation 3:1 – Revelation 5:14

Day_____ Revelation 6:1 – Revelation 8:13

Day_____ Revelation 9:1 – Revelation 11:19

Day_____ Revelation 12:1 – Revelation 13:18

Day_____ Revelation 14:1 – Revelation 16:21

Day_____ Revelation 17:1 – Revelation 18:24

Day_____ Revelation 19:1 – Revelation 20:15

Open Plan

Reading time 15 minutes each day

Old Testament.

Summarize the past seven day's evening:

_____
_____
_____
_____

A verse you would like to remember:

_____
_____
_____
_____

Month _____

Open Plan

Reading time 15 minutes each day

Old Testament.

Summarize the past seven day's evening:

_____

_____

_____

_____

A verse you would like to remember:

_____

_____

_____

_____

REVIEW ANSWERS

(1) Page 31 Things you have seen.
  Things that are now happening. Things that will happen later.

(2) page 30 = Revelation

  Blessed is he who reads and those who hear the words of this prophecy, and keep those things which are written in it, for the time is near.
  (Revelation 1:3 NKJV)

(3) Page 29 Letters
(4) Page 30 books of
  James, 1Peter, 2Peter, 1John, 2John, 3John, and Jude

(5) Page 23
  Does it come from God?
  Was it written by a man of God?
  Does it tell the truth about God?

(6) Pages 25, 26, 27, 28.
  39 books

(7) Page 25. Old Testament
  Genesis, Exodus, Leviticus,
  Numbers, and Deuteronomy

(8) Page 28. New Testament
  Matthew, Mark, Luke, John

(9) Page 21. Greek
(10) Page 21. Hebrew

EXERCISE

(1) New Testament
Book of 2 Timothy
Chapter 2, Verse 15
Key word, Worker

(2) Be diligent to present yourself approved to God, a worker who does not need to be ashamed, rightly dividing the word of truth.
(This is the NKJ Version.)
(Your version may use other words.)

(3) 2 Timothy 1:1. Paul an apostle
(4) 2 Timothy 1:2. Timothy
(5) Encouragement, be strong. (You summarize?)
(6) Matthew 3:16
(7) Mark 1:10, John 1:32
(8) King James Version
(9) Page 49 Be consistent
Study The Bible in context
Know who is speaking
Know who is being spoken to
Know the subject of the speaker

BIBLIOGRAPHY

The Nelson Study Bible (New King James Version).
Thomas Nelson, Inc ., 1997.

Holman Bible Dictionary. Holman Bible Publishers, 1991.

The Nelson Study Bible (New King James Version).
Thomas Nelson, Inc ., 1997.

Odle, Joe T. Church Member's Handbook Broadman Press, 1962.

The Open Bible (New Living Translation) Thomas Nelson, Inc 1998.

The Nelson Study Bible (New King James Version). Thomas Nelson,
    Inc ., 1997.

Zondervan Interactive Software. Zondervan Publishing House.

This book is design to give youth and young adults a better understanding of <u>The Bible</u> and guide them toward a comfortable relationship with <u>God</u> and the Church.

+ **Basic Christian Training is simple and to the point, without any long, flashy dialogue .**
+ **From the Beginning sheds light on Bible history and its transformation through the centuries.**
+ **This book puts the new believers and pastors on the same page, from the Beginning.**
+ **From the Beginning is about building your own relationship with God.**

About the Author

Burdon Campbell, was born in Houston Texas, and he was raised in Los Angeles, California from an early age. He graduated from John C. Fremont High School, and then studied two years at Los Angeles Trade Technical Junior College to become an electrician. He joined the United States Air Force, became a civil engineer electrician, and later an aircraft electrician. Burdon served 20 years in the United States Air Force, The Air Force gave him the opportunity to visit the ruins of ancient cities in Greece, Egypt and Libya. He stood on the same rock (The Areopagus) where The Apostle Paul preached, visited the Red Sea (The Gulf of Suez), and toured the ancient city of Sabratha (west of Tripoli). These experiences increased his interest in Bible history. Burdon fell in love and married a Baptist girl named Mary from Jackson, Mississippi. They have been married for 58 years. They have one son, two granddaughters, one great grandson, and one great granddaughter. Burdon is currently a member of Faith Fellowship Community Church in North Highlands, California. He taught a Bible study at Folsom State Prison for five years. He also serves his church, his community, and his city as a caring, humble, and respected deacon.